Leonardo DiCaprio

Unofficial & unauthorised by Charlotte Grainger

OMNIBUS PRESS

In the space of four short years Leonardo DiCaprio has gone from being Hollywood's hottest young talent to the brightest star in the known universe.

At the age of 23, the *Titanic* golden boy has achieved the kind of success and adulation most actors can scarcely dream of, the kind of success that even in the dream factory known as Hollywood they would be hard pressed to make up.

He is the star of the most expensive, most successful film of all time.

His stunning good looks, coupled with a quite extraordinary natural acting ability make him that rarest of breeds – a certifiable star.

"That kid, he has 24 carat gold charisma," says Leonardo's *Man In The Iron Mask* director Randall Wallace, "he's amazing."

What makes Leonardo's meteroic rise all the more amazing is that it's richly deserved. What's even more amazing, is that his rags-to-riches story of a talented, handsome young kid raised on the wrong side of the Hollywood tracks who grows up wanting to be a film star and finally makes it in Tinseltown, is the kind you only see in the movies.

His stunning performance as Romeo in Baz Luhrman's dazzling modern retelling of Shakespeare's classic love story *Romeo & Juliet* finally made Leonardo into an A-list commodity and a bankable name. However, his portrayal of the struggling artist Jack Dawson, who slips aboard the *Titanic* just before it sets off, wins the heart of Kate Winslet's repressed Rose, and later dies an icy death in the freezing cold waters of the Atlantic, has captured the hearts of millions around the world. Forget the special effects, forget the huge budget, without Leonardo, without his blue-green eyes, his foppish blond hair, his classical good looks, *Titanic* just wouldn't float.

Prior to starring in *Titanic*, Leonardo had tended to concern himself more with playing oddballs, misfits and troubled, tormented teenagers, rather than the headline-grabbing, limelight-hogging, star-making, heroic leading man roles that many of his contemporaries had chased after.

He had preferred to challenge himself as an actor first and foremost, learning his craft, rather than set himself up as a star, choosing to play a gay French poet or a drug-addicted teenager instead of, say, Batman's leather-clad sidekick.

It's this attitude and mindset, a desire for longevity, coupled with an immense, natural talent, that has set Leonardo apart from the chasing Hollywood pack, and earnt him an Oscar nomination at the age of nineteen for his extraordinary performance as Johnny Depp's mentally-retarded brother Arnie in *What's Eating Gilbert Grape?*

But he couldn't escape his destiny.

Leonardo was destined to be a huge star.

Four years later and Leonardo is Hollywood's golden child. His mere presence is enough to send women into hysteria the world over. His name a guarantee of bums on seats. His presence in a film a seal of quality. He is this generation's pin-up. All those who've met him vouch to his charm, his engaging personality, his goofy sense of humour.

He is a star who parties hard, and lives life to the full. As with his acting, Leonardo refuses to compromise in his off-screen life. "He's a hell of a guy," says his *Mask* co-star Jeremy Irons, "a wonderful talent."

Leonardo Wilhelm DiCaprio was born in Los Angeles on November 11, 1974, the son of an Italian-American father, George, and a German-born mother, Irmalin. Both hippies, they met at college and separated before Leonardo was even born, but didn't divorce until a few years later. They named their son after the man responsible for painting the Mona Lisa, following a visit to a museum in Florence, Italy. Standing before a Da Vinci painting, Irmalin felt her unborn son kick inside the womb. "My dad's like, 'It's a sign! His name's Leonardo!'," Leonardo told one interviewer. "'He's kicking at the Leonardo Da Vinci painting! His name's Leonardo'." Despite his parents' separation, Leonardo's childhood was, he says, a very happy one. In the hope of disrupting their son's upbringing as little as possible, his parents remained close friends, meaning Leonardo spent as much time with his father – a leading underground figure in New York in the mid-60s – as he did with his mother. He has remained close to his parents, and both are instrumental in the direction of Leonardo's career. "My parents are so a part of my life, they're like my legs or something," he says.

Raised in one of Los Angeles' poorest districts, an area known as "Syringe Alley", off the famed Hollywood Boulevard, Leonardo was, as a child, witness to the worst side of the Hollywood dream, with drug addicts and prostitutes lining the streets outside his home. It's an experience that has stayed with him to this day. "It was a bit of a shock. My mom took great care of me, but I was able to see stuff at an early age, see the distinctions, and it's like, yeah, okay, life is crap," he says. "I would walk to my playground and see, like, a guy open up his trench coat with a thousand syringes. I saw some major homosexual activity outside my friend's balcony when I was five." Later, Leonardo and his mother moved to a ranch house in the more salubrious Los Angeles neighbourhood of Los Feliz, where Leonardo was still living until very recently.

Fittingly for a kid growing up in the showbiz capital of the world, Leonardo was a born entertainer, hogging the limelight whenever possible, a personality trait which, coupled with his gift for mimicry – his Michael Jackson impressions were a big hit at school – earned him many friends and made him a natural performer. While Leonardo didn't excel at school, he would spend his time watching movies, especially those of his favourite actors, Robert De Niro and Al Pacino, dreaming that he could play their roles. Less than a decade later, he would be acting opposite De Niro himself...

Although Leonardo made his first television appearance aged five on a kids' show called *Romper Room* – and was thrown off the set for unruly behaviour – it was almost a decade later before he decided he wanted to be an actor, a decision, he admits, which was almost purely financial. By now, Leonardo's father, George, had remarried, presenting Leo with a stepbrother, Adam Starr, a child actor who had earnt $50,000 for starring in a TV commercial for a breakfast cereal. "It kept going through my head: my brother has $50,000!" remembers Leo. "That kept on being my driving force. I just remember for, like, five years thinking my brother was better than me because he had that."

Inspired by his stepbrother's financial success, Leonardo took the first steps on the long road that would eventually lead him to stardom: that of getting himself an agent. Alas, it was not, as he discovered, an easy task. He was turned down by several agencies until one of his mother's friends put him in touch with a talent agent where she worked. And so, at the age of 14, Leonardo DiCaprio finally made his acting debut in a television commercial for Matchbox cars, later going on to appear in nearly two dozen adverts and short educational films.

Around this time an agent suggested that Leonardo DiCaprio was, maybe, too exotic name, and was perhaps preventing him from getting certain roles. Thus, for a brief period Leonardo DiCaprio became Lenny Williams, a move which, not surprisingly, didn't seem to make him any more employable. Reverting to his birth name, Leonardo soon got the break he had been waiting for, a role in a two-part episode of *Lassie*.

For the next few years, television was to be Leonardo's drama school. He continued to make a steady stream of guest appearances on a number of television shows, including *Roseanne* and the TV spinoff of the movie *The Outsiders*, before, aged fifteen, he joined the cast of top US soap *Santa Barbara*, where he got his first opportunity to play the kind of tortured teenager, in this case an alcoholic, that would later to make his name in Hollywood.

Lolitaesque thriller *Poison Ivy*. The film also starred *E.T.*'s Drew Barrymore in her comeback role following her battle with alcohol and drug addiction, and Sara Gilbert from TV's *Roseanne* with whom Leo had become friends with while guesting on the show. The closing credits list Leonardo simply as "Guy" and if you look closely he can briefly be seen dressed in denim in the film's opening sequence, one of a group of teenagers standing over the body of a dog which has been recently run over.

Alas, it was not to be the film that would make Hollywood sit up and take notice of the young DiCaprio. That would come along soon enough, however – Leonardo finally waved episodic television goodbye in 1992 when he auditioned for the role of the young Tobias Wolff in Michael Caton-Jones' *This Boy's Life*, giving him the chance to play opposite his great hero, Robert De Niro.

For many aspiring young actors, auditioning with the legendary Oscar-winning star of *Raging Bull*, *GoodFellas* and *Cape Fear* would have been an intimidating experience. Not Leonardo who took the whole thing in his stride, a reflection of the laid back manner he'd inherited from his father. "He was doing karate kicks in the hallway. He wasn't serious at all," recalls Leonardo's best friend Tobey Maguire, himself an actor who starred most recently in *The Ice Storm* with Sigourney Weaver and who was also at the audition.

"*I* stood up in front of De Niro really forcefully and I pointed at his face and screamed one of the lines sat there and waited for a reaction," laughs Leonardo. "I remember De Niro had this smirk on his face, like, obviously (he knew) this kid wanted to come in here and show him that he had guts. Everyone started laughing and I said, 'What? What is it?' And, well, the cool thing is that I obviously showed him something." Indeed he did. But director Michael Caton-Jones had auditioned Leonardo early on in his search for an actor to play Toby and although he was blown away by Leonardo's reading was loathe to cast one of the first actors he had seen. Caton-Jones embarked on a four-month casting trip which took in most of the US and Canada. But as time went on, it became clear that nobody matched up to Leonardo's powerful reading with De Niro – he won out over 400 other hopefuls for the role that would make him a star.

Based on Wolff's autobiographical novel, *This Boy's Life* was an intense family drama. The plot centred on the mental and physical abuse suffered by the young Toby Wolff (Leonardo) at the hands of his monstrous stepfather, played by Robert De Niro, as he attempts to instil in Toby his distorted sense of right and wrong.

It was a difficult role for any actor to play not least one as inexperienced as DiCaprio, not only in terms of the enormous amount of emotional acting required, but also in terms of requiring him to be faithful to a character who was actually a real person.

"*This* role was different from any other I had played," said Leonardo who gratefully accepted all the on-the-set tuition his much more experienced co-star was willing to offer. "This was something that was true, that actually happened to this guy. When you're in the moment of a powerful story like that, you can't help but feel emotionally disrupted."

While the film wasn't a box office success, taking less than $5 million, Leonardo's performance was too sensational to go unnoticed, and won him the New Generation Award from the Los Angeles Film Critics Association. Moreover, all of Hollywood was starting to recognise the immense talent waiting to be tapped in this young actor.

Hollywood didn't have long to wait to see what this new kid on the block could really do. In his next film, *What's Eating Gilbert Grape?*, Leonardo was cast as Johnny Depp's mentally retarded brother Arnie. While the film was fundamentally the story of Depp's character – stuck in a small, dead-end town, taking care of his housebound mother and brother (Leonardo), and dreaming of getting out – it was Leonardo who wound up stealing the film with a tremendously soul-searching performance. Depp, like Leonardo, had first found fame as a heartthrob on TV, turning his back on teen stardom, establishing himself to be a fine, immensely talented young actor with a series of quirky, brave choices, including *Edward Scissorhands* and *Cry-Baby*, which had finally helped people see past his natural good looks. Ironically, Leonardo almost didn't get the part of Arnie because he was considered too handsome. "I needed someone who wasn't good looking," insists the film's Swedish director Lasse Hallestrom whose *My Life As A Dog* won the Golden Globe for Best Foreign Language Film in 1989, "but of all the actors who auditioned for the role of Arnie, Leonardo was the most observant."

Leonardo is an avowed critic of the method approach of acting favoured by De Niro among others – "I would have a nervous breakdown if I had to go through a movie for three months and be that character on and off set. I know what I'm doing but when they say 'Cut', I'm fine. I can joke around. I don't go hide in a corner and yell at anyone who tries to speak to me" – but he made an exception in this case. Having made Hallestrom's shortlist for Arnie, Leonardo immersed himself in the role, not only watching videos of mentally impaired children as research, but also by visiting them, studying the characters, mannerisms and personality traits, trying to get inside them and therefore inside the character of Arnie.

"*I* really wanted to get that feeling of a four-year-old child, with the whole world open to him, rather than the sort of depressing sort of retarded character that you feel sorry for," says Leonardo. "People have these expectations that mentally-retarded people are really crazy, but it's not so. It's refreshing to see them because everything's new to them. Playing Arnie was fun because everything I did was spontaneous."

His mesmerising portrayal of Arnie was in stark contrast to Depp's solemn, internal performance, and upon the film's release, Leonardo again found himself singled out for praise, winning several critics awards including his second New Generation gong. But the icing on the cake was being nominated for an Oscar for Best Supporting Actor – aged just nineteen. He was in exhaulted company, competing against John Malkovich, Tommy Lee Jones, Ralph Fiennes, and Pete Postlethwaite. Actors playing disabled roles had traditionally done well at the Oscars – Dustin Hoffman for *Rain Man*, Daniel Day-Lewis for *My Left Foot* and Tom Hanks in *Forrest Gump* being three of the most notable and recent examples – though on this occasion Leonardo lost out to Tommy Lee Jones for his performance in *The Fugitive*. "Nobody was happier for him than me, that's the f*****g truth," reflected Leonardo whose own triumph at the Oscars is surely only a matter of time.

With the Oscar nomination, Leonardo DiCaprio had well and truly arrived. Suddenly he was being hailed as Hollywood's hottest talent and offered every young male role in town, including that of the ultimate young Hollywood star in a James Dean biopic. He demurred. Yet having finally made the impact in movies he had long dreamed of, Leonardo was uncertain of what direction his career should take. "I didn't know where I was gonna go as an actor so I didn't know what type of movies I wanted to do. I just felt like doing a movie is doing a movie. I get money and fame and that's great, and I can act and that's fun."

He was loathe to choose any of the big-budget studio movies being offered him, turning down a role opposite Bette Midler in *Hocus Pocus*. "I don't want to do big box office just yet," he said at the time. "The more you stay low key at a young age, the more you have room for that stuff in the future, and as long as a I can maintain doing films that I want to do, then I'd rather not blow my load on the work. It seems that a lot of people who try to do that disappear."

With that in mind, he also passed on the role of Robin in *Batman Forever* that would eventually go to Chris O'Donnell. "I couldn't deal with playing a character who rides motorcycles and has a leather jacket and is a tough kid, you know?" says Leonardo. "There's the stamp of stereotypical right there. It's like, can you think of anything more obvious?"

Leonardo

DiCaprio

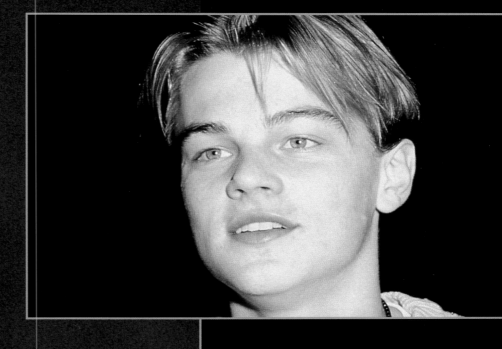

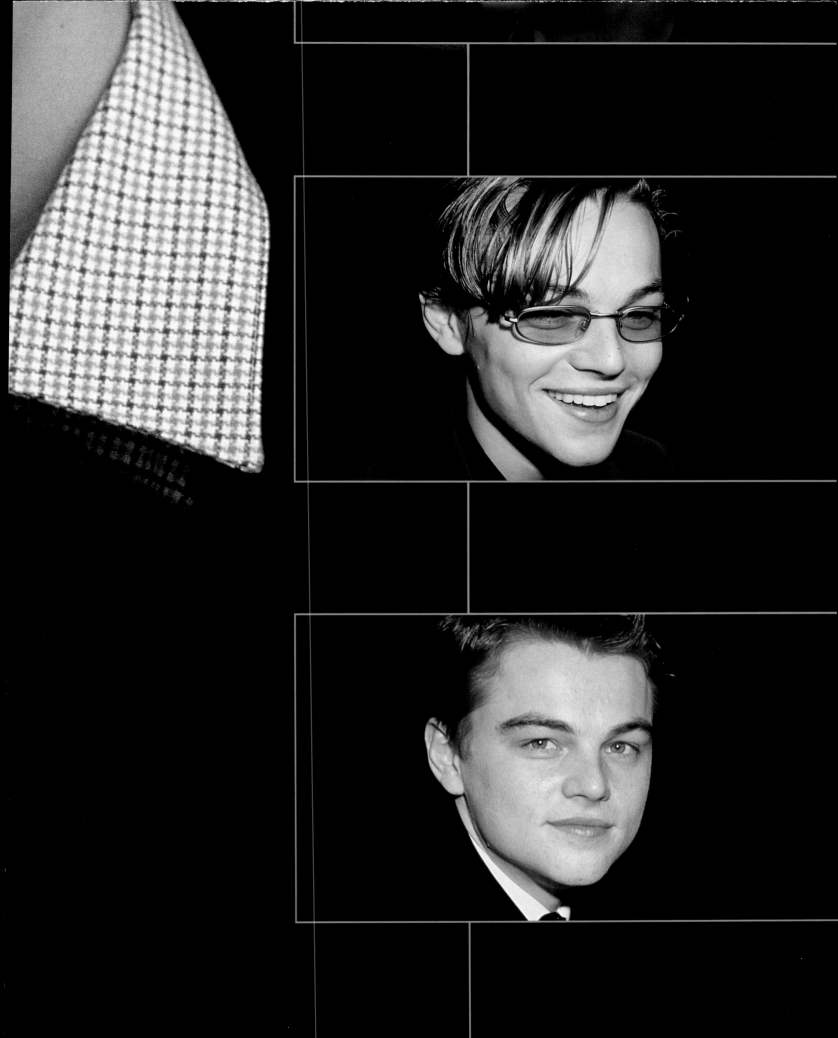

One role that interested him, however, was that of the interviewer in Neil Jordan's *Interview With The Vampire*. The part had originally been mooted for River Phoenix, an actor Leonardo had often been compared to and had long admired. Phoenix's promising career had been cut tragically short when he collapsed and died of an overdose outside The Viper Room, a Los Angeles nightclub co-owned by Johnny Depp. Leonardo auditioned for the role but was ultimately considered too young – the part eventually went to Christian Slater.

Leonardo's leaning towards the less obvious led to his next outing, *The Foot Shooting Party*. This rarely seen 27-minute short, directed by Annette Haywood-Carter, was commissioned by Disney as part of its strategy to help encourage potential new directors with no behind-the-camera experience. It starred Leonardo, in hair extensions and bellbottoms, as a Seventies rock'n'roll singer who shoots himself in the foot to avoid going to Vietnam.

More widely seen – though not by as many as its makers had probably hoped – was *The Quick And The Dead* in which Leonardo starred opposite Sharon Stone. Director Sam (*The Evil Dead*) Raimi's stylish homage to spaghetti westerns, the film revolved around a gunfighting contest presided over by mayor Gene Hackman in the desert town of Redemption. The part was that of a fresh-faced gunfighter named The Kid, who, it transpires, is Hackman's character's son. Leonardo had already turned down the role several times, uncertain about starring in a western. "Everyone around me was saying, 'This is a good movie.' I had this thing about not doing big commercial movies because most of the mainstream movies are just pieces of garbage." With the producers already to go with another actor, they gave Leonardo one last call. "With one day to decide I said, 'Okay, I like Sam Raimi and this character's really funny and cool.'" Stone, a co-producer of the film, was so insistent that Leonardo co-star alongside her, that she wound up paying for half of his salary out of her own pocket.

Despite some fanciful and innovative direction from Sam Raimi and a terrific cast that included Russell Crowe and Lance Henriksen, in addition to Stone, Hackman and DiCaprio, the film was not the hoped for box office success. Although the film itself was critically maligned, Leonardo predictably escaped any bad press, his performance again garnering the most positive reviews. "I don't regret it," he says now. "It's not my favourite film in the world. I guess it was not that good. I had a good time doing the character."

Not even the failure of *The Quick and The Dead* would prove capa[ble] of upsetting the Leonardo bandwagon. Directors were still eager to u[se] young star and even before The Quick and The Dead opened, Leona[rdo] had already finished work on his next feature, in which he played an[other] of his troubled teen roles. Based on Jim Carroll's autobiographical m[emoir] *The Basketball Diaries* told of a group of Catholic teenagers' descent [into] drugs and crime. The material had long been considered risky subjec[t] for a movie, although at various stages a number of hot young actors [had] been attached to the project including Matt Dillon and River Phoen[ix].

Leonardo's attraction to the project was immediate. "*The Basketba[ll ...]* was the first time where I actually read a script and I didn't want to [put it] down." Leonardo saw the film as both an opportunity to make a stat[ement] against drugs and to experience the horrors of drugs without actually indulging himself. He spent much time researching the role with a d[rug] counsellor, as well as the real-life Jim Carroll, investing what he learn[t into] his performance, and later accompanying Carroll on a book signing [tour].

Leonardo's co-star in the film was former rap singer and Calvin Kl[ein] model Mark Wahlberg otherwise known as Marky Mark. When the [idea] of Wahlberg was first muted, Leonardo freaked. He told the first-tim[e] director, Scott Kalvert – a pop video veteran with several Marky Ma[rk videos] to his credit – "No, no, no, absolutely not. But as soon as he came i[n he was] really cool and he did the scene and I couldn't help be charmed by w[hat he] did. He brought an element of being truly street, because that what [he is]. He was the best person for the job."

The pair became close friends, often hanging out at night after film[ing in] New York clubs. Before long, this earnt Leonardo a reputation in the [media] as a party animal – a claim he has always disputed. "I'm written abo[ut in] tabloids because I go out places," he said at the time. "Most famous [people] aren't out and about. I'm a 22-year-old guy who wants to live out his [life] and do films at the same time. Having fun is a priority to me."

The tabloids also took issue with his convincing portrayal of Carr[oll's] drug-addiction, so much so that it was suggested he was actually doi[ng drugs] while making the film. "I don't do drugs and never have," he insiste[d,] a statement that makes his convincing performance in the film even [the] more impressive.

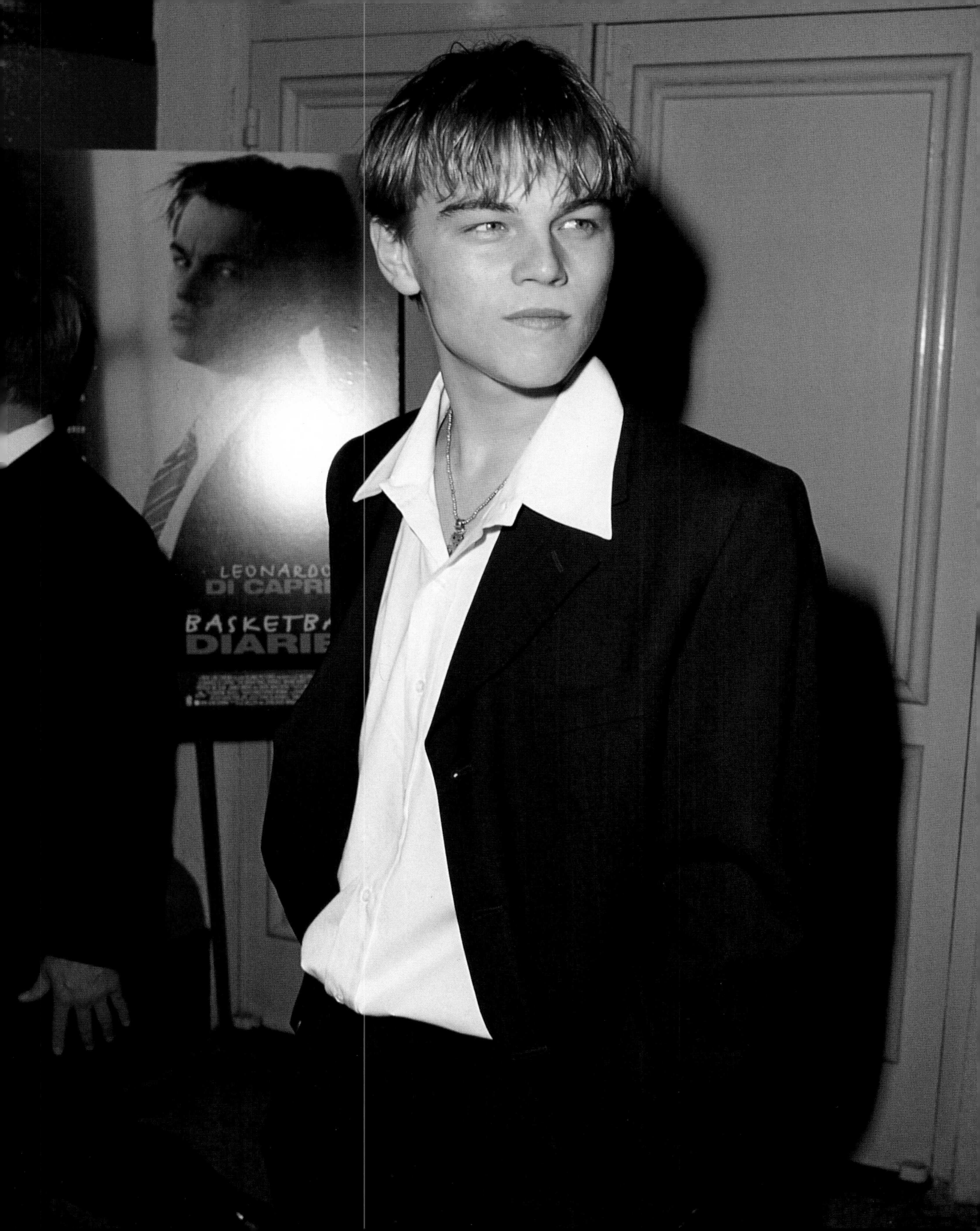
LEONARDO

Unfortunately, while critics once again waxed lyrical over Leonardo's stunning work as the drug-stricken Jim Carroll, the film itself failed to make much of an impression at the box office, due in part to its dark tone and controversial subject matter.

If playing a teenage junkie sucked into crime and turning tricks was considered a risk, Leonardo's choice for next role as French poet Arthur Rimbaud would seem to suggest that here was an actor who would only consider the most controversial of roles. The subject matter of *Total Eclipse* – Rimbaud's homosexual, ultimately self-destructive relationship with the married writer Paul Verlaine (played by David Thewlis) – was enough to have Leonardo's advisors warn him against taking on the part. But Leonardo called it one of the most important roles of his career, requiring from him another emotionally intense performance. Yet all press attention was focussed not on his acting ability but on the fact that he was required to kiss Thewlis onscreen.

"*I* got very nauseous, as it was my first time kissing a guy. It was like slow motion. I saw his lips coming towards mine and I was like, Oh Jesus, is this really going to happen? Like, enough talking about it: my lips are going to touch yours". The scene was clearly a problematic one for Leonardo; he later commented "I'm sorry. Call me homophobic if you like, but I'm just grossed out by it". His attitude led to accusations of homophobia from his co-star Thewlis, although it's worth pointing out that Leonardo had, to a lesser degree, touched upon similar material in both *This Boy's Life* and *The Basketball Diaries*.

The film, like *The Basketball Diaries* before it, was not a success, and although Leonardo's remarkable performance inevitably won much critical praise, he found himself for the first time in his career on the end of a few less than flattering reviews. "I think the only people who liked *Total Eclipse* were people who liked Rimbaud. But then a lot of people who liked Rimbuad hated it too," Leonardo commented afterwards. While he was in France filming *Total Eclipse*, DiCaprio also found time to make a brief appearance alongside Gérard Depardieu, Harrison Ford and Robert De Niro in *Les Cent Et Une Nuits*, a film about the centenary of cinema, directed by Agnes Varda.

During the filming of *This Boy's Life*, De Niro had presented Leonardo with the script for *Marvin's Room*, a film he intended to produce. The young star was thus re-united with De Niro in Jerry Zaks' adaptation of Scott McPherson's acclaimed stage play. The story of two sisters, played by Meryl Streep and Diane Keaton, *Marvin's Room* again featured Leonardo as a troubled teenager. He played Streep's son Hank, who is responsible for burning down their house; coming after two starring roles in a row, the film was something of a relief for Leonardo. His co-star Keaton enthused warmly over the young DiCaprio's merits: "I was in love with him," she gushed. 'He's beautiful. So talented. So gifted and funny – everything you want in a person. He's like a light – he walks in and it's like magic. Meryl Streep and I would sit there and go, 'God, this kid is so beautiful.'"

"He's so delicious as a person," agrees Streep. "I got jealous when he did his scenes with Diane; he clearly liked her character better. He liked teasing Diane and making her giggle."

If there was ever an actor born to play William Shakespeare's tormented over Romeo, it's Leonardo DiCaprio. But just like his role in *The Quick And The Dead*, Leonardo initially took some persuading to sign on. "I didn't want to run around in tights, swinging a sword," said Leonardo, "I wouldn't have done it if it was a period piece." Australian director Baz Luhrmann who had scored an impressive debut with *Strictly Ballroom* had been looking for a fitting follow up when he hit upon the idea of a radical reinterpretion of Shakespeare's classic play for the MTV generation, a colourful, vibrant, resolutely sexy take of the oft-told tale, replacing swords with guns and relocating the plot from the play's Verona, Italy to Verona Beach, USA. In his search for the ideal Romeo, Luhrmann came across a photograph of Leonardo in a magazine and instantly knew he was the perfect choice. Moreover, Leonardo's clout could get the film financied. The next step was to find a Juliet. All of Hollywood's hottest young actresses dutifully filed in to audition, but none had what Luhrmann wanted until Leonardo mentioned Claire Danes' name to his director after seeing her on TV. The pair were ideally suited. Danes, like Leonardo, had started out in television and won an Emmy for her cult series *My So Called Life*, before moving into movies with *Little Women*, *Home For The Holidays* and *How To Make An American Quilt*.

Juliet

Filming took place over three months in Mexico City and was hardly a stroll in the park. The production was plagued by bees, storms and both stars were struck down with dysentry. To relieve the tension, DiCaprio, who has it written in his contract that he can fly in a certain number of friends to hang out on set, shipped in a few and partied. At other times he would simply indulge in his gift for mimicry, with his Michael Jackson impersonation making regular appearances. During filming, Leonardo and Danes became close, but, despite rumours to the contrary, were never more than friends. "I think they had crushes on one another," says their co-star John Leguizamo," but they kept it very professional. Nothing was ever done."

In fact, Danes found him something of an enigma: "I spent four months with him and I couldn't figure him out," she admits. "I still can't figure out whether he's really transparent or incredibly complex. I think he's the latter, but I don't know."

With its hip soundtrack, MTV style visuals and hot young stars, *Romeo & Juliet* opened at number one at the US box office, going on to make $50 million; not bad for a film that cost $15 million. It put DiCaprio on the A-list and made his reputation as a bankable star, one of only a handful of under 25-year-old film stars capable of opening a movie. But even its troubled production and subsequent box office success couldn't have prepared Leonardo for what was to come, as he signed on board the good ship *Titanic*.

"*The* curious thing is I actually didn't want Leo at first," says *Titanic*'s writer-director James Cameron of his decision to cast DiCaprio as struggling artist Jack. "Leo was recommended by the studios, as were other young, hot actors. He didn't strike me as necessarily having the qualities I wanted for my Jack."

Despite his reservations, Cameron met with the young star and was immediately won over. "I basically just loved him," says Cameron. "He can quickly charm a group of people without doing anything obvious... the second I met him I was convinced."

While Leonardo had always been wary of making a big, commercial movie, he says it was the story and character not the size of the production that appealed to him: "It was something that I probably would have done if it was commercial or not." Yet it took his English co-star Kate Winslet to finally persuaded him to say yes. Both attended the 1996 Cannes Film Festival; Winslet discovered where Leonardo was staying and turned up at his hotel. "I was thinking, 'I'm going to persuade him to do this because I'm not doing it without him, and that's all there is to it," she remembers. "'I will have him because he is f*****g brilliant. He's a f*****g genius."

Winslet's badgering worked. DiCaprio signed onboard *Titanic*, receiving his first million dollar pay cheque. But little did he know what he was letting himself in for. To accomodate the sheer scale of *Titanic's* production, a purpose-built studio complex was constructed in Mexico where cast and crew began work on a life-size replica of the original ship. Indeed, so huge was the production it took two Hollywood studios, Fox and Paramount, to stomp up the film's budget which ultimately swelled to $200million, making it the costliest film ever made.

With a director as legendary for his perfectionism as James Cameron at the helm, it was not going to be an easy shoot, and as *Titanic's* budget ballooned so did the schedule. During the intense seven months of filming, Leonardo and Winslet became incredibly close. Again, as with *Romeo & Juliet*, the rumour mill suggested that Leonardo and his co-star were more than friends. The pair insist they were more brother and sister, helping carry each other through the trials and tribulations of filming. "They were really there for each other," remarks director James Cameron; "She was my best friend for seven months," says Leo. "We were kind of the two goofy kids on the set," says Winslet. "Y'know, working with Leonardo DiCaprio – he's a bit gorgeous, and I was worried that I was going to be bowled over by him. But the second we met we just clicked." Sharing the same gross out sense of humour probably helped. "He'd be tickling me, groping me, winding me up. And I'd be doing the same thing back, sort of grabbing his bum," reveals Winslet.

Titanic finally arrived in US cinemas five months late, but even with the wealth of negative publicity that it had accumulated through its troubled production, it's proved to be the film they couldn't sink, having so far over taken $1 billion worldwide. It is now the most successful film of all time; nominated for a record-breaking fourteen Oscars, it eventually won eleven of them, including that of Best Film, equalling the all-time record set by *Ben Hur* back in 1960. And although Leonardo himself wasn't nominated, there is little doubt that much of the film's continuing success is due to multitude of female fans around the world returning time and time again to watch their hero fall in love on the high seas.

Those Leonardo fans clamouring for a fresh fix of their hero were served well by *The Man In The Iron Mask* in which their hero appears not once, but twice, as the vainglorious King Louis XIV of France and his imprisoned twin brother Phillippe. Filmed immediately after *Titanic* wrapped, this clunky, often laughable adaptation of the classic novel by Alexandre Dumas, directed by *Braveheart*'s screenwriter Randall Wallace, provided Leonardo with his weakest, least convincing role(s) to date, but its success has served only to further underline his superstar status.

"*I* was really exhausted after *Titanic* but it was a situation that was too good to be true," says Leonardo who admits the opportunity to work with John Malkovich, Gérard Depardieu, Gabriel Byrne and Jeremy Irons, who play Dumas' legendary quartet of musketeers, was too good to pass up.

When the film opened in America in March 1998 in direct competition to the all powerful *Titanic* which had remained at the top spot since its release in December 1997, both films tied for first place at the box office – a truly unique situation for a truly unique actor.

With the record-breaking success of *Titanic*, the adulation of millions of fans around the world, and a truly gifted acting talent, Leonardo DiCaprio literally has the world at his feet. Still only 23, he is probably the most in demand, most photographed, most written about celebrity in the world today, with interest in his love life, his liasions with various supermodels or his relationships with his co-stars now front page news across the globe.

But what next for the young star who has spent the best part of the last nine years working solidly? He's been inundated with scripts, but early indications are that he may be finally slowing down. He's talked about his desire to make just one film a year, to take some time off and travel, to live the normal life of a 23-year-old, albeit a 23-year-old whose fee for a movie has skyrocketed to $20million.

In the meantime, we'll have to make do with his role in Woody Allen's upcoming *Celebrity*, as well his part in a short film called *Don's Plum*, that he made prior to *Romeo & Juliet* for friends which, for various reasons, may or may not be released.

Whatever he chooses to do, let's hope he's not gone from our screens for too long...

Leonardo...

+ *Mum*   + *Mark Wahlberg*   + *Kristine Zang*

+ Tommy Hilfiger

+ Sean Penn

+ Claire Danes

+ Billy Zane

+ Kate Winslet

Filmography

Critters 3 *1991* *Directed by* Kristine Peterson

Poison Ivy *1992* *Directed by* Katt Shea Ruben

This Boy's Life *1993* *Directed by* Michael Caton-Jones

What's Eating Gilbert Grape? *1993* *Directed by* Lasse Hallestrom

The Foot Shooting Party *1994* *Directed by* Annette Haywood-Carter

The Quick And The Dead *1994* *Directed by* Sam Raimi

The Basketball Diaries *1995* *Directed by* Scott Kalvert

Total Eclipse *1995* *Directed by* Agnieskka Holland

Les Cent Et Une Nuits/One Hundred And One Nights *1995* *Directed by* Agnes Varda

Marvin's Room *1996* *Directed by* Jerry Zaks

William Shakespeare's Romeo & Juliet *1996* *Directed by* Baz Luhrmann

Titanic *1997* *Directed by* James Cameron

The Man In The Iron Mask *1998* *Directed by* Randall Wallace

Awaiting release:

Don's Plum *1995*

Celebrity *1998* *Directed by* Woody Allen